MARTIN ROXON

Keys For Inspiring A Successful Living: The Fastest Steps For Survival, Resilience And Redemption

Table of contents

Introduction

This Book, *keys for inspiring a successful Living: the fastest steps for Survival, Resilience and Redemption* highlight the roles that success plays in life, the impact of success and how it got to affect you and your acts.

The advantage of success is so important in your life that you can not do without success. This Book explores all the characteristics, features, attributes and the relationship that exists between success and you in effect that you will live a successful, happy, healthy, prosperous, long life in the World. I bet; you can not wait to explore all the keys that lead to a dream able life that you have been waiting for. The principles that will help you become the person you wish or desire to become in life are all loaded inside this book. Learning the act of developing and inspiring the spirit of Survival, Resilience and Redemption in life can make you achieve whatever you want in life. I am convinced to believe that this book is for you "A matter of adjustment makes a lot of difference".

Chapter 1

How to seek the right knowledge

People who are nature-like are always curious, excited about life, and wanting to know more. They embrace the unknown and want to feel more knowledgeable about the world. They do things like learning foreign languages, reading books and the papers, and watching exciting films. They are excited about other cultures and want to learn about them, and they are well-informed and confident in their views while being able to admit when they want to know more about something. It's this thirst for knowledge that will keep you excited about life, and will make you want to live on in spite of adversity.
The more you know, the more equipped you feel to deal with a major setback or challenge.

Nature is the natural, physical or material world or universe. Nature also refers to   phenomenal of physical world and also to life in general.

See, (Genesis 1:1) "In the beginning God created the heavens and the Earth"

From the practical perspective of things, you can see that nature has parts.
The Sun, Trees, Grass, Flowers, Animals, Birds, Rivers, Oceans, Moon, Star, seas etc which makes up the beautiful nature you see around you, are all created by God.

Nature- like people are always asking questions when they are faced with a new situation. Ask questions until you feel like you have a firm grasp of a situation instead of feeling immobile and unable to deal with it.

Matthias Claudius wrote a hymn called: we plough the fields, and scatter.

And in that hymn he said: "All good gifts around us are sent from heaven above"……..

That is a replica reflection of the creativity of God. Nature also has life that keeps them in existence. You can notice this as you touch and feel the natural environment or surroundings.
The mineral resource existed because it has a lot to do with you, same also with the Sun, Trees, Grass, Flowers, Animals, Birds, Rivers, Oceans, Moon, Star, Seas etc.
Success is important for inspiring the natural living that will bring about the fastest steps for Survival, Resilience and Redemption that you need in life.

See (Jeremiah 29:11) "for I know the plans I have for you says the Lord, plans for welfare and not for evil, to give you a future and a hope"

Nothing existed before God did His wonderful creation, which marks the beginning and existence of everything else including man in the World.
Without success in your life, it would have been difficult for you to survive on this planet earth. This is true as you feed from the natural environment in which you live or dwell. And the reason for this; is to give you a hope and a feature.

Did you feel happy for this honest revelation?

I can guaranty you that with this shared truth of God being the creator of everything, a depressed man in a perfect reflection of nature and success, can renovate and rebuild his inner consciousness about life, knowing that everything existed for a purpose. The point is that, getting to know how things begin or come into existence can change your own perception of life from wrong to good.

Anne Frank Said: "the best remedy for those who are afraid, lonely or unhappy is to go outside, somewhere where they can be quite alone with the heavens, nature and God. Because only then does one feels that all is as it should be and that God wishes to see people happy, amidst the simple beauty of nature. As long as this exists and it certainly always will I know that then there will always be comfort for every sorrow, whatever the circumstances maybe and I firmly believe that nature brings solace in all troubles"……

The above verse from Anne Frank is a fascinating life changing keys for inspiring a natural living and making your living easy and successful. That also tells you that life is visually and completely empty without success.
I am of the opinion that you cannot do without success, and I also have the strongest believe that you can be great, powerful, and transformed in life, notwithstanding what you are going through right now.

Keys to make your living easy

Avoid gossips and backbiting talks

Show love and kindness to people

Learn to be discipline in life

Create more time for yourself

Develop a cheerful happy lifestyle

Avoid living a trouble lifestyle

Be satisfy with the resources God has given you

Live, work and start with your God given resources or gifts

Get your life fully transformed now! God bless you!

Chapter 2

How to make your living easy

Going through means of living has become a major issue in the society today. I was arguing with my very good friend on a sunny day, and it was as if the sun wants to come down on us. And suddenly my friend exclaimed!
What kind of Nature is this?
This question infant attracted my attention very much, as he asked a very clear question that requires an explanation. I replied what do you mean, as he seriously asked: where the hell does this sun come from?
It sounds funny right! But the fact is that he asked a very serious question.
May I remind you that for the purpose and benefits of this book in the feature that you ought to know more about nature and success, and how it affects your life? This is because other people may not know deep about their natural environment and its successful importance to them.

In our daily lives, we often rush through tasks, trying to get them done, trying to finish as much as we can each day, and speeding along in our cars to our next destination, rushing to do what we need to do there, and then leaving so that we can speed to our next destination.
Unfortunately, it's often not until we approach our final destination that we realize what madness this all is. At the end of the day, we're often exhausted and stressed out from the grind and the chaos and the business of the day. We don't have time for what's important to us, for what we really want to be doing, for spending time with loved ones, for doing things we're passionate about.
It doesn't have to be that way. It's possible to live an easy life, one where you enjoy each activity, where you are

present in everything (or most things) you do, where you are content rather than rushing to finish things. Here are some steps to live a simple, peaceful, content and easy life.

Decide what is important

Take a step back and think about what's important to you. What do you really want to be doing, who do you want to spend your time with, what do you want to accomplish with your work? Make a short list of 4-5 things for your life, 4-5 people you want to spend time with, 4-5 things you'd like to accomplish at work.

Examine your commitments

A big part of the problem is that our lives are way too full. We can't possibly do everything we have committed to doing, and we certainly can't enjoy it if we're trying to do everything. Accept that you can't do everything, know that you want to do what's important to you, and try to eliminate the commitments that aren't as important.

Do less each day

Don't fill your day up with things to do. You will end up rushing to do them all. If you normally try (and fail) to do 7-10 things, do 3 important ones instead (with 3 smaller items to do if you get those three done). This will give you time to do what you need to do, and not rush.

Leave space between tasks or appointments

Another mistake is trying to schedule things back-to-back. This leaves no cushion in case things take longer than we planned (which they always do), and it also gives us a feeling of being rushed and stressed throughout the day. Instead, leave a good-sized gap between your appointments or tasks, allowing you to focus more on each one, and have a transition time between them.

Eliminate as much as possible from your to-do list

You can't do everything on your to-do list. Even if you could, more things will come up. As much as you can, simplify your to-do list down to the essentials. This allows you to rush less and focus more on what's important.

Slow down and enjoy every task

This is the most important tip in this article. Read it twice. Whatever you're doing, whether it's a work task, eating, brushing your teeth, cooking dinner, driving to work: slow down. Try to enjoy whatever you're doing. Try to pay attention, instead of thinking about other things.

Be in the moment

This isn't easy, as you will often forget, but find a way to remind yourself. Unless the task involves actual pain, anything can be enjoyable if you give it the proper attention.

Eat slowly

This is just a more specific application of taking things more slowly but it's something we do every day, so it deserves special attention.

Drive more slowly

Another application of the same principle, driving is something we do that's often mindless and rushed. Instead, slow down and enjoy the journey.

Lemony Snicket said: "even though there are no ways of knowing for sure, there are ways of knowing for pretty sure"..........

Chapter 3

Life in the garden

Remembering the beautiful life you enjoy and experience while relaxing in the garden will help you appreciate the values and attributes of nature and success. In order to unlock the potential keys that will inspire the successful living, and the fastest steps for survival, resilience and redemption; you need to reflect and recreate through your natural environment.

God placing man in the garden called "garden of Eden" is His way of showing his outmost love and care for you, that He (God) wants you to be happy, successful, joyful, healthy, prosperous etc.

See (Genesis 2:15) "the Lord God took the man and put him in the Garden of Eden to till it and keep it."

God is wise because he knows that you need the garden to grow, develop and expand. For God to place man in the garden, instructing him to take charge; has a couple of reason. And that is the reasons why you need to love and care for your natural surroundings or environment.

The evolutionary theory of life shows that you need nature in order to survive, because you grow and develop with your natural environment. And this has led me to coin up what I believe to be the key Evolutionary stages of life.

Steps to Survival

Steps to Resilience

Steps to Redemption

Chapter 4

Steps to survival

Deciding what to do

Quickly think about all possible options and be decisive about what the best survival course of action is. For example, if you think the best survival course of action is to seek out help and civilization, don't wait four or five days before you come to this conclusion. Take action on the first or second day if possible, while you still have strength and endurance working for you.

This is also the steps where you can use the natural environment as means for you to survive, this is not like the survival of the fittest, but is more or less like fun for you to live a natural life, especially when you are not matured in brain and technical know-how. I believe that in this stage, you have to resort more to your natural environment in order to be able to survive. Surviving here includes: good health, happiness, joy, success, and prosperity etc. these will help you get readings, meanings and interpretation of life from the natural environment in which you live.

Learn to embrace change

One major aspect of being more surviving minded is learning to deal with and accept change. Studies show that if you view the changes in your life as challenges instead of threats, you will be much more equipped to deal with them. Learning to adapt to new situations, whether it's moving to a new place or becoming a new parent, is a survival skill that will help you find creative solutions to new problems and to face adversity with relative calm and ease. If you're stuck in your old ways and can't imagine doing things any way but your way, then you're bound to run into trouble sooner or later.

Work on being more open-minded. Stop judging people for how they look, what they do, or what they believe. Not only will this help you learn something new, but being aware of a variety of perspectives can help you see the world in a new way if you're forced into an unfamiliar situation.

Another way to get better at embracing change is to always be trying new things, whether you're making new friends, picking up a new painting class, or reading a new genre of books. Keeping things fresh can make you less resistant to change.

Seven key steps to survival

Create Your Plan

Prepare Your Space

Know What You Have and What You Need

Set Your Budget

Start Saving and Storing

Get Your Survival Gear Together

Practice and Prepare

Chapter 5

Steps to resilience

"Changing Your Thoughts, Changing Your Actions, Staying Strong"

I believe that: Here is where you have made little development in brains and technical know-how. You can make fire and tools for yourself, in order to feed and warm yourself, cultivate and plant in the garden or hunt animals etc. As you feed and grow in your environment or surroundings; in some points you may be seen chasing animals like monkeys, while in some other points you may be seen climbing mountains. And these exercises are necessary in order for you to live and appreciate life.

Resilience is the ability to bounce back from tough situations and to avoid becoming a victim of helplessness. Being resilient can help you manage stress, lower your chances of depression, and it has even been proven to make people live longer. You may feel like you've had so much bad luck that it's impossible to come out strong on the other end, but your lack of control stops here. Once you learn to seize your life by the reins and prepare for the unexpected, you'll be on your way to being a more resilient person -- and to living a happier, more purpose-filled life as a result.

Key steps to resilience

Develop a more positive attitude

Improve your problem-solving approaches

Learn from your mistakes

Don't fall victim to learned helplessness

Meditate

See a doctor if you feel incapable of coping

Find purpose in life

Maintain a strong social network

Find a mentor

Take care of yourself

Work toward your goals

Be a person of action

Do yoga

Stay physically fit

Accept the things that happen to you

Maintain your self-esteem

Nourish your creativity

Manage your stress

Make peace with your past

Develop a more positive attitude

Sure, it's not easy to have a positive attitude when you broke your arm in a car accident that wasn't your fault, or when you've been rejected by the last five girls you've dated. It's not easy -- but that doesn't mean it's impossible. Your ability to be optimistic and to see your setbacks as isolated incidents instead of indicators of your future success is precisely what will make you succeed in the future. Tell yourself that just your positive attitude alone has the ability to help you seize more opportunities be creative about ways to improve your life, and to feel more fulfilled overall.

Find a way to nip your negative thoughts in the bud. Any time you notice that you think or feel something negative, try to think of three positive thoughts to fight those negative ones.

You know what will go a long way in helping you be more positive? Hanging out with positive people. Positive attitudes, just like negative attitudes, are infectious, so spend more time with people who see opportunity at every turn instead of whiners and complainers, and pretty soon, you'll be noticing the change within yourself.

Stop procrastinating: Though something truly awful may have happened to you, chances are it's not the end of the world. Your problems are as big as you make them out to be.

Improve your problem-solving approaches

Part of the reason some people struggle with being resilient is because they don't know how to face their problems. If you develop a workable method of dealing with challenges, you'll be more likely to feel capable of solving them and of not feeling hopeless. Here is a helpful approach for dealing with a problem in front of you:

Understand the problem first. You may feel that you're unhappy with your job because you're not being paid enough, but if you dig deep, you may see that it's really because you feel that you aren't following your passion; this presents an entirely new set of problems than the one you thought you were faced with originally.

Find more than one solution. Be creative. If you think there's only one solution to the problem -- quit your job and start trying to play in a band full-time -- then you'll run into issues because your approach may not be practical, doable, or it may not be able to make you happy in the long run. Make a list of all of the solutions and pick your top 2-3 candidates.

Put it into action: Evaluate your solution and see how much it was able to help you succeed. Don't be afraid to get some feedback. If it didn't work out, don't look at it as a failure, but as a learning experience.

Learn from your mistakes

Another quality of resilient people is their ability to learn from their mistakes. People who are not resilient make the same mistake again and again because they are unwilling to be honest about why they failed in the first place; people who are resilient take the time to think about what didn't work so they can avoid running into the same kind of trouble in the future. Don't feel depressed after rejection or failure -- no matter how much it hurts -- and think about how it can help you grow stronger instead.

As the saying goes, "A clever man learns from his mistakes. A wise man knows how to avoid them." Though you can't avoid your first mistakes, you can gain the wisdom that will help you not to make the same ones in the future.

Look for patterns of behavior. Maybe your last three relationships haven't failed just because of bad luck, but because you've failed to invest the necessary time into them, or because you keep trying to date the same type of person, who just may not be compatible with you in the end.

Don't fall victim to learned helplessness

A person who is not resilient faces a setback and tends to think that it happened because he or she is somehow unworthy, that the world is unfair, and that things will always be that way. Well, if that's your attitude, then this will become the truth; if you don't want to be a victim, then you have to look at setbacks and think that they happened because of an unfortunate situation, not because it was 100% your fault, because you had some bad luck, not because the world is a terrible place, and see that it won't always pan out this way. Here's an example:

Let's say Marcia is a talented actress who has not been called back after her last thirty auditions. If she's not resilient, she'll think, "I wasn't called back because I'm not talented or pretty enough. The acting industry is impossible to break into if you don't have the right connections. I might as well give up because that will never change."

If she is resilient, however, she'll look at it this way: "Sure, I wasn't called back after my last thirty auditions, but the competition was tough, and I know I could have done better for some of them. Though becoming a successful actress is difficult, it's not impossible to make it without connections. If I keep trying, something is bound to work out for me."

Meditate

Meditating can help you clear your mind, lower stress, and feel more ready to face the day and any challenges ahead of you. Studies also show that just 10 minutes of meditation can make you feel as rested as getting another hour of sleep, as well as making you feel more relaxed and able to cope with your problems. One of the reasons you may not feel capable of dealing with the world is because you feel overwhelmed, burnt out; meditating can help you slow down and feel in control of your situation.
Just find a comfortable seat and close your eyes, focusing on the breath rising in and out of your body. Work on relaxing your body one part at a time. Block out any noise or distractions.

See a doctor if you feel incapable of coping

It is important to have talked through the problems you're facing with someone who is in a position to help you make sound decisions about seeking therapy, using medicinal options, and finding any other sources of support that you may need. While you can face difficulties yourself, it's important to talk to a doctor to make sure you're doing so the best way possible.

Seeing a doctor is not a sign of weakness; admitting that you may need some help actually takes a lot of strength.

Find purpose in life

Having a goal and dreams increases resilience. Simply bumbling along and letting life take you wherever it will reduces resilience and leaves you open to, poor life choices, and being a doormat. It reduces your sense of control over your life, which easily leads to and anxiety.

Consider what goals you have, whether little or large. These goals give a sense of purpose to your life and keep you focused.

Learn to recognize what gives you a sense of purpose in life and what detracts from that. Live your life in accordance with your values and convictions.

Maintain a strong social network

While it's easy to let go of important relationships in our frenetic lives, it is important to make room for them. Good relationships are a pillar of rock for resilience and are a source of support when the times get tough. Maintain your family and friend relationships and you'll have an instant, trustworthy and reliable support network around you at all times.

One study of 3,000 nurses with breast cancer showed that the nurses with 10 or more close friends were four times more likely to survive than those without.

Find a mentor

Another way to develop your resiliency is to find a mentor who can help you deal with the blows that life throws at you. This can be a person who is succeeding in your field, a grandparent, an older friend, or really anyone who can help you achieve your goals and face adversity with a level head. You may feel that your life is hopeless and that life is caving in all around you, and having an older and wiser person who has been there can help you feel like you're not alone and like you're equipped to deal with life's challenges.

Take care of yourself

You may be so busy dealing with a serious break-up, a job loss, or another significant event in your life that you don't have time to shower or get more than a few hours of sleep a night. However, if you want to be mentally strong, then you have to be physically able, too. If your body is in a funk or you're just feeling unkempt, then you'll be even less equipped to deal with the challenges. No matter how awful you're feeling need to make an effort to shower, brush your teeth, sleep, and get into a normal routine, so that you can start feeling as "normal" as you can.
Make sure to make time for mental breaks when you're caring for yourself, too. Studies show that taking mental breaks, whether you're just daydreaming or closing your eyes and listening to a song that you love, can help ward

off those stress chemicals and will prevent you from feeling overwhelmed.

Work toward your goals

If you want to be a more resilient person, then you have to not only set goals, but you have to work to achieve them. If you're just sitting around waiting for life to happen to you or dealing with pain and suffering caused by another person, then your levels of resilience will only go down. Making a plan to achieve your goals -- whether you're getting an advanced degree, getting more physically fit, or trying to get over a break up -- will help you feel directed, focused, and driven.
Make a week-by-week, or month-by-month plan for getting what you want. Though life is unpredictable and you can't plan everything, setting out some sort of a plan can help you feel more in control of the situation, and more likely to succeed.

Tell other people about the goals you want to achieve. Just talking about your goals and discussing what you're going to do will make you feel more obligated to achieve them.

Be a person of action

Don't be the guy or girl who sits around complaining about how life is unfair or wishing that things happened differently. Sure, it sucks that you've been working on a novel for ten years and nobody wants to publish it. It's not fair that you got fired for something that wasn't your fault while everyone else in your office is still spending their Christmas bonuses. But does that mean you're going to sit around moping and wishing that things had turned out differently? Absolutely not -- you're going to do something about it.

If nobody wants to publish your novel, that doesn't mean you have to let your worth lie in what other people think about your work. Be proud of yourself for a job well done and go write another one.

If you got fired, pick yourself up and look for another job -- or even consider finding a job that gives you more value and makes you happier, even if you take your career down a new path. Though it may not feel like it, getting fired may be the best thing that ever happened to you, even if it absolutely doesn't feel that way at the moment.

Do yoga

A study from Harvard Medical School showed that people who do yoga as opposed to other forms of physical fitness were less prone to angry outbursts and more capable of dealing with challenging. When you do yoga, you will strike challenging poses and will learn to build strength and endurance in holding the poses even when your body is begging you to stop; this builds up your ability to "stick with" challenging situations and to find the resources to stay calm and determined.

Stay physically fit

Though you don't need to have six pack abs to deal with a major crisis, being physically strong certainly helps. If your body is stronger, then you have build up the strength and endurance to have a stronger mind and it will indeed help you in moments of crisis. Being physically fit will improve your self-esteem, positive thinking, and ability to feel empowered, all of which will help you be resilient. Even something simple like taking a walk in the sunshine for twenty minutes a day has been proven to help people be more open-minded and ready to face challenges.

Accept the things that happen to you

It isn't possible to foresee the things life has in reserve for us. Expecting life to be always peachy or always dreadful is a way of viewing life in extremes and will cause you to have unrealistic expectations. You cannot always predict how you'll respond to unseen painful events but you can use resilience as the means to build up defenses that will help you get through the worst without falling apart completely. In nurturing resilience, your quality of life will improve.

Maintain your self-esteem

Your self-esteem depends, among other things, on how you value yourself. It's important to form a positive perspective about yourself and about life in general to ensure resilience. In acquiring competencies and responsibilities, you nourish your self-esteem, so it is important to get involved in life and not withdraw into yourself and feel threatened. If you feel that you are worthless, then you will feel incapable of tackling challenges.

Seek value through using your talents and abilities to their fullest, be it in a professional, volunteer, business, home front, or other capacity.

Learn new abilities and skills as often as you can. This will strengthen your self-esteem and can also ward off fears. For example, if you're afraid your children might be hurt some day, take a first aid course to reduce your sense of fear and to increase your confidence in being able to cope should something happen.

Workshops, seminars, courses, etc., are all good ways to improve your knowledge and to expand your network of acquaintances on which you can draw support if needed.

Nourish your creativity

Creativity is an expression of yourself and the way in which you live. Creativity lets you unleash what words or conversation cannot express or even understand. Read How to crank up your creativity for ideas on how to nourish your creative side. Nourishing your creativity can also help you be more creative when finding more solutions to problems, and will show you that you can look at the world in more than one way.

Take a photography class, write a poem, take up watercolor painting, redecorate your room in an original way, or consider sewing your own clothes.

Manage your stress

While it can be difficult to stay calm during times of hardship and worry, the stress impedes your ability to remain resilient. Managing stress will allow you to tackle to difficulties with greater serenity and focused thinking instead of burying yourself down deeper and trying to hide.

Make stress management a priority, no matter how busy you are. If you are overbooked and under slept, see if there are any commitments you can cut back on.

Feeling stressed and overwhelmed by your everyday life will make more likely to not be able to accept new stresses or challenges that arise because you'll feel like you don't have enough room for them in your life.

Indulge in activities that let you completely unwind. Give yourself that space and peace to relax regularly, thereby giving your resilience a chance to increase.

Make peace with your past

It's important to unravel past motivations that feed into current approaches to life. Until you make peace with the hardships of the past, they will continue to influence and even direct your current responses. This is a total loss of resilience. See a therapist, a counselor, or your doctor if you cannot work through past issues alone or with friends or family. It is vital to let go of the emotions and binds that have followed you into the present and that cause you harm. Don't expect this to happen overnight but do tackle it; the end result will be a far more resilient self.

Think about past setbacks that made you feel like your life was over. See how you were able to work through them -- and to come out stronger on the other side.

If you feel like you're missing closure on an event from your past, do whatever you have to do to be able to move on from it, so you can feel stronger when addressing future challenges.

Chapter 6

Steps to redemption

Seeing your way to redemption

The theme of seeing God-or not seeing God-recurs
throughout Parashat Vayeira. But seeing God in this
Genesis context bears little relation to what today we might
consider "spiritual experience"-radical amazement, or
transcendence. To the contrary, each time the Hebrew
root reish-alef-hei is employed in Vayeira, it offers us a
model of seeing God in the earthly substance that surrounds
us each day. To see God in this instance opens us up to
possibility, even (or especially) in the direst circumstances
when paths to redemption are concealed. The human
capacity to see God in the physical substance of our daily
lives is necessary, we learn from Vayeira, and linked in an
almost frighteningly direct way to human survival itself.
The stakes are indeed high, for at least in this narrative,
where there is a refusal to see, a turning away from, or
blindness to God, death and destruction soon follow. The
reader then notes who is blind to God, who averts her eyes,
and who develops the capacity to see.
Vayeira begins with a visit of angels, or messengers, to
Abraham and Sarah and the subsequent birth of Isaac;
the Akeidah tale concludes the parashah. The stories
bracketed in between-those of Sodom and Gomorrah, and
the expulsion of Ishmael-portray characters with vastly
different ways of seeing. The men of Sodom and
Gomorrah, for example, attempt to rape Lot's visitors,
revealing their refusal to see any aspect of the Divine in
their human guests. They are subsequently cast with a

blindness that leaves them helpless to find their way, and they are ultimately consumed in the destruction of the two cities.

Hagar, too, in very different circumstances, initially declines to see. Instead she averts her eyes from her dying child Ishmael, perhaps hoping that if she refuses to see God in her suffering child, then she and the child both might be spared. But unlike the men of Sodom and Gomorrah, Hagar is anything but blind, and ultimately she is compelled to turn toward her son with open eyes. And when she does look toward her dying child, she sees a way to alter his tragic fate. She spots a well, and she acts; giving the boy water, she saves his life and enables him and his descendants to become a people. Hagar, by seeing, transforms the course of human destiny.

Later in the text, Abraham too seems initially unable to see; so caught up is he in fastening his son to the altar that he nearly misses the signal God sends to prevent him from slaughtering his son. Yet, he does manage to look. And when he does, he sees the ram that will replace his son on the altar. Seeing, Abraham is able to fashion for himself a way out of the "bind" he has created.

Through Hagar's actions and those of Abraham as well, the message of Vayeira is one of hope: God is manifest in all things, and we need only allow ourselves to look. Unlike the men of Sodom and Gomorrah, Abraham and Hagar (and elsewhere in the parashah, Lot and Sarah) actively cast their eyes about and see God in their surroundings: in strangers walking down the road, in the deepest well and the highest mountaintop, and in the struggle of a tiny ram trying to extricate its curled horns from a thicket. And they act with urgency, moving desperately to ensure their own survival. At the start of Vayeira, Abraham hastens to perform the mitzvah of hachnasat orchim, hospitality; Hagar gives the boy water to drink; Abraham and Isaac ascend the mountain; and finally, Abraham offers the ram in place of his son. In each case, the act of seeing enables our characters to steer away from impending doom and move toward salvation instead.

Through the act of looking and seeing, we open a realm of possible paths not readily apparent when we objectify and take for granted all that fills our daily surroundings-the people, animals, and natural resources with which this earth is blessed. Vayeira reminds that even in the most desperate of circumstances, we must open our eyes and look about us. Recognizing God in all creation, we may have the capacity to act with urgency to ensure our survival.

By the way to redemption

I believe that people are moving from theism to pantheism. There are some who don't like the word pantheism, the idea that God is everything. They prefer the word panentheism, which means that God is in everything. I, however, don't think that the distinction is real. (Zalman Schachter Shalomi, Wrapped in a Holy Flame: Teachings and Tales of the Hasidic Masters.

Rabbi Meir says: Do not look at the flask but rather at what it   contains.

Seek Adonai while He can be found, call to Him while He is near. (Isaiah 55:6)

Your guide to redemption

Where do you find God? Rabbi Zalman Schachter Shalomi posits the possibility that everything is God. To use Rabbi Meir's terms, do you believe that God is the flask or only that which it contains? The question suggests a distinction between body and spirit. Do you accept a body or spirit dichotomy, or do you take Schachter Shalomi's more wholistic approach? How might a pantheist perspective alter the way we treat our bodies, fellow human beings, and the earth around us? Why has our tradition been so wary toward traditional notions of pantheism?

If we saw things differently-perhaps viewing all that surround us as sacred-would we act with greater urgency, as did Hagar and Abraham in Vayeira? Would this perspective make new possibilities apparent in your personal life? Thinking more globally, what if our leaders saw God in all substances on earth? Might they act with greater urgency to make peace and to save the planet from environmental devastation?

Have you ever witnessed something that immediately compelled you to act? How can we teach ourselves, and our children, to see the way toward new possibilities that might ensure our survival-individually, as a people, as a planet?

I also believe that this is where you have been redeemed fully, all you have to do, is to develop more in brains and technical-know how. Your growth in wisdom enables you to take care of animals in the garden, prune the flowers, and also take care of yourself with the natural endowments that surround you. Etc. you can live a healthy, successful, prosperous, joyful and happy life, as you travel or go out on vacations or holidays to enjoy and play with animals, birds, and sometime swim in the river or take a walk in the woods etc. this will always help you to get the peace, comfort, healing and joy that you need.

I believe that the average common man ought to have thank God for loving him so much. This is a fact; as God has given you charge and dominion over nature.

See (Genesis 1:28) "And God blessed them, and God said to them, "Be fruitful and multiply, and fill the earth and subdue it; and have dominion over the fish of the sea and over the birds of the air and over every living thing that moves upon the earth".

The above verse simply pointed out the powerful keys you possess in life to unlock supernatural victories.
Nothing in life happened by chance, but they happened because they are necessary.

For example, I may not be the best inspiration or motivational writer in the world, but the fact that you are reading this book now makes it necessary.

The natural environment you see around you, such as the pasture, garden, weather, mountains etc. are all there for you. Get use to it, learn to cherish them and they will help you a lot in life. There is nothing you cannot find with nature, e.g. life, love, blessing, joy, prosperity, good health, success. Etc. Robert Frost wrote a poem:

"God made a beauteous garden
With lovely flowers strown
But one straight
Narrow pathway
That was not over grown
And to his beauteous garden
He brought mankind to live
And said "to you,
Children
These lovely flowers I give
Prune ye my vines and fig trees
With care my flowers tend
But keep the path way open
Your home is at the end"

The above poem is a perfect reflection of the beautiful life offered to you by God through nature. And you can only help by protecting it from destruction.

Chapter 7

How to inspire people

I will also like to talk about some of the inseparable attributes of nature and you. These inseparable attributes of nature, if properly study can be used by you to develop some of the powerful principles about life. And these principles are what I called "the way life ought to be"
The principles that I have developed will help you position yourself to prosper in life; with the entire guild you will need to succeed.
"The way life ought to be" is my own way of defining prosperity as possessing all that God promised in his words. The principles which I have developed to help you appreciate the meaning of life are as follows:

Focused

In order to inspire people, you must possess an extraordinary amount of focus. It's important to eliminate distractions from the work area and to hone in on the key issues at hand. While inspiring people are often pulled in numerous directions simultaneously, they must be able to retain clear minds and focus on the things that matter.

Passionate

It's possible to teach someone to be inspiring or influential, but truly effective people are already passionate about what they do. Your enthusiasm and level of commitment can inspire people and motivate them to do better work.

Modeling the attitude you want each person to have is one of the most effective ways to lead your team toward a successful destination.

Assertive

As a person, you have requirements for the people around you and goals that must be fulfilled. When people aren't meeting expectations, you must feel comfortable being assertive. Assertive people are firm and bold, unafraid to go after what they want. Such a level of certainty and confidence will serve both you and your team well as you tackle larger challenges and go after new goals.

Decisive

People are often called on to make big decisions, so it's also important for you to be decisive. Of course, a decisive person should never be confused with an impulsive one. A decisive person carefully weighs the potential effects of each option and chooses the opportunity that works best for his or her team. To be decisive, you must also feel comfortable taking responsibility for the results of your choice.

Empowering

Supporting people is one of the best ways to encourage people to perform well. Empower each individual by making it clear that you trust his or her judgment. Give people the authority they need to do their jobs well and show them an appropriate level of respect.

Confident

Successful and inspiring people are confident in their own abilities and decisions. If you want other people to believe in your capability as an inspiring or influential person you must first believe in yourself. While you should make sure your confidence isn't perceived as arrogance, there's nothing wrong with feeling a strong sense of certainty about your choices.

Communicative

Always keep your people informed about what's going on. All too often, leaders leave their team members out of important discussions and meetings. A lack of communication promotes the spread of false information and resentment among your team members.

Self-Aware

It can be tough to retain a strong sense of yourself and the way you appear to others, but focus on being self-aware. Consider your strengths and weaknesses as objectively as possible and don't be afraid to ask for feedback on your performance.

Humble

Inspiring people are down-to-earth and easy to relate with. People feel more comfortable connecting with an inspiring or influential person who is humble and compassionate. Strive to understand where other people are coming from and keep a healthy, grounded perspective on your own achievements.

Honest

Finally, inspiring or influential people are honest. Be upfront with the people around you and trust them enough to communicate openly and authentically together. It's important to build a level of mutual trust within your team so that each person feels comfortable addressing his or her concerns with you.

Chapter 8

Principles of living (101)

The lilies

A fundament understanding of this principle or attribute will give you the starting point in life and how you need to live your life. The life you live today does not depend on the money and wealth you have acquired but on God only.
See (Matt. 6: 28) "And why are you anxious about clothing? Consider the lilies of the field, how they grow; they neither toil nor spin;"

In the life span of the lilies, you will be able to identify one or two attribute which they possess that is similar to yours. For example, the lilies lives and grows, you on the other hand also lives and grows.

Jesus said: how they grow, they neither toil nor spin, yet I tell you, even Solomon in all his glory was not arrayed like one of these. (Matt. 6: 28).

The message here is, if the lilies which neither toil nor spin, but shared some attributes with you, can be arrayed by God with every thing it needs to grow in the field. Then how much value is you than the lilies of the field which today is alive and tomorrow is thrown into the oven.

See, I have grown to a point in my life that I can't just do things that need to be done; I need to know if it works.

Albert Emstein said: "there are only two ways to live your life. One is as though nothing is a miracle. The other is as though everything is a miracle"…

I believe that you are free to live a much happier and zero anxious life on earth than the lilies of the field. This is because you are more valuable in the sight of God than the lilies of the field. Yes, this is true because God loves you so much that he gave up his only son for you.

See (John 3:16) "for God so love the world, that he gave his only son, that whoever believes in him should not perish but have eternal life".

I can guaranty you that; the proper reflections on how the lilies of the fields grow will help you develop sound principles, that will completely reduce your stress or anxiety and restores happiness, joy and good health to you. Anxiety and worries brings sadness to a person's life. But one thing is sure, that you can't keep concentrating on those things that brings you down but on those things that will rise you up. You need to create and develop a stable manner approach in order to live the higher life that you desired.

Chapter 9

The principles of living (102)

The sparrows

This principle is more practical in terms of life span, as the attributes of the sparrows are more similar to yours.
But what does the bible reveal about this principle. See (Matt. 6:26) "Look at the birds of the air, they neither grow nor reap nor gather into burns, and yet your heavenly father feeds them. Are you not of more value than they?"

The above, is from the Holy book of life, where you can find the truth and answers to every thing in life. The sparrows have legs, ears, eyes etc. you on the other hand possess this same qualities.

But the bible said "Look at the birds… are you not of more value than they?"

The word "look" requires you to pay serious attention to facts. Because, you bring nothing into this world and you are not going to take anything out of it.
The birds of the air have legs, ears, eyes etc. but they neither sow nor reap nor gather into barns and yet God feeds and take care of them. Thank God today that you have a God that takes you serous. And I also want you to know that the facts that God loves and care about you are still there today.

See (1 peter 5: 7) "cast all your anxieties on him, for he cares about you"

With a clear understanding of this principle, you will see that your life does not depend on your legs, ears, eyes or anything that you have here on earth but on God.

So, neither your ability nor disability of sowing nor reaping nor gathering can stop God from providing for your needs. He is willing and able to do abundantly and above all you can ask of him.

See (Ephesians 3:20) "Now to him who by the power at work within us is able to do far more abundantly than all we ask or think".

It is important to note as a fact that God want you to stop worrying about life, because He is able to feed you as he did for the sparrows.

So many people have always asked me, how can they live a natural life? And they kept receiving the same answer from me; which is "trust in God". I remember a young beautiful young looking lady who came into my office on a Friday afternoon for counseling, she said: I am tired and confused in life and suddenly boost into tears, I look at her, pointing through the glass windows to the beautiful looking garden flowers around my office building and said, look at those beautiful looking young flowers, does it look like to you, the God who made them and made you is tired and confused, she said no! I said why? She said because they look very beautiful out there. I said: correct!

Now the reasons for all these stories, is because I want you to look at your natural environment whenever you are depressed and put a smile on your face, not only putting a smile on your face, but also thank God for giving you life; so that you can live with purpose.

See (psalm 139: 14) I praise thee, for thou art fearful and wonderful. Wonderful are thy works! Thou knowest me right well".

I may not know what you are going through right now, but whatever the case may be, just like the young beautiful looking lady in my office, I want you to look at your natural environment and get your joy, happiness, dreams and revelation back. And most importantly; give God the praise and glory for all the things he has done for you.
You can not get the best of life by worrying too much. So, to stay focused in life you have to believe the fact that God said he is able. This is not about what you can do, but about what God can do for you.

Douglas Adams once said: "I may not have gone where I intended to go, but I think I have ended up where I needed to be"

Nature always has a way to humble you, and also honor you in life; so, you have to be careful and also tread carefully with your life.

I also want you to think about great man, such as Jacob, David, Sampson, Solomon, Abraham, Job etc. who have conquered and accomplished so many things in life through these keys that has inspired the natural living in their life's, which I believe is the fastest steps for Survival, Resilience, and Redemption.

Chapter 10

How to identify your right season

I want to use this chapter to discuss about seasons as regards to nature and how it affects your life.

I don't know if you have experience bad or good season moment in your life? Whether yes or no! I will show you how you can live in bad or good seasons that will come your way and use them to make extra ordinary achievements.

This Seasons God has given to you through nature together with the keys and secretes of unlocking all the supernatural and divine blessings that comes with them are real and practical.

Stay with me, and this is big! because this is your time and your life is about to experience the most powerful turning point that you could ever imagine at the end of this practical facts and revelation you are about to get.

I will discuss two seasons and how you can make it applicable to your life.

See (Ecclesiastes 3: 1) "For everything there is a season, and a time for every matter under heaven:"
Season may be a period of time when a particular activity happens or a particular thing is done.

The secretes to Plenty and abundance

This season called season of plenty is always very critical in life at times, because of the temptation that will come against you when you have plenty and abundance. The grace to resist temptation in this time, will determine the success you make with your wealth or plenty. This is because so many people self destroyed the plenty they have with their own hands, by investing in things that are going down, rather than investing in things that are going up. And that is because they may feel that they have enough and so fail to plan for the feature ahead.

You can not see your season of plenty as some thing that will be enabling your mentality to think that there is; no more challenges for you to solve. You must always pray and prepare more in your time of plenty because "new levels bring new devils"......TD Jakes

See (Philippians 4:11-12) "Not that I complain of want; for I have learned, in whatever state I am, to be content. I Know how to be abased, and I know how to abound; in any and all circumstances, I have learned the secret of facing plenty and hunger, abundance and want."

The time when you should remain more focused, in order to re-dedicate and recommit yourself to God, is the time when you have plenty and abundance. In order not, to waste your resources in things that are not profitable, you need to invest in God's kingdom. Your case could be the case of a man who has plenty today and begs tomorrow because of too many lapses or mistakes in life.

I am of the opinion that your last mistake should be your stepping stones. Learn from it and see where you have failed, then solve the problems and make it applicable to your life. You can as while give to God when you have, because this will keep you and give you more wealth to invest and spend. Remember, a giver does not lack.

Chapter 11

Keys to plenty

Give and always acknowledge God for given you

Don't lose focus, but be strong and willed in your endeavors

Develop a sound investment and reinvestment policy for yourself

Make use of your time wisely

Remember to empower others

Always remember that God is your source to every thing

Learn how to entrust and save your resources in God

Preparing for time and season before they approach your life is also a key to make remarkable difference out of the season. Your experience will depend on how prepared you are before the season. This is because man is subject to change, and the life you live is driven by challenges. Your life is bound to season of plenty designed or destined to you by God.

See (Genesis 41: 33-36) "Now therefore let pharaoh a man discreet and wise, and set him over the land of Egypt. Let pharaoh proceed to appoint overseers over the land, and take the fifth part of the produce of the land of Egypt during the seven plenteous years."

Change is good, but failing to plan is not a good approach to life. In order to inspire the natural living, which is the fastest steps to Survival, Resilience and Redemption, you need to start planning and seeking the right way now. For example, you can start planning for your new car, house, office, education, business and family etc. before you enter your new seasons of plenty.

How to avoid lack

The lack season does not naturally look like the world is about to end, as you may see it, but is a season that comes with divine intervention, inspiration and creativity in life.
The worries that God has made it possible for you to experience hard times and difficulties, does not mean that your life is over.

As my friend will always say; Challenges are there to make us strong. Yes! Because you only have to get into speed and think what ways to make things right in your difficult times. It may be that you have suffered a lot, but that does not mean that you should lose faith in God, as every trouble and temptation comes with a way of escape.

See (1 Corinthians 10:13) "no temptation has overtaken you that is not common to man. God is faithful, and he will not let you be tempted beyond your strength, but with the temptation will also provide the way of escape, that you may be able to endure it"

Cultivate your sense of humor

Hard times call for looking at the lighter side. Humor helps you to gain perspective during hard times; it also improves your sense of well being through an increase in dopamine levels. Watch a comedy, read a funny book, and spend time around people who are genuinely funny. When going through hardships, be sure to balance your sorrowful movies, books, and thoughts, with funny, humorous ones, to prevent you from hitting the bottom of the pit of despair.

Learn to laugh at yourself. The ability to not take yourself so seriously will make it much easier to face challenges with a smile on your face.

It only takes a disciplinary mind to realize, see and solve problems in a difficult period or time. This is because it takes nothing to be poor but takes something to be rich and discipline.

Your quest for survival should be able to make you develop a set of principles or goals that will allow you live "don't worry be happy life that you desire".

Bobby McFerrin wrote a song titled: "don't worry! Be happy" and in that song he said: "in every life we have some trouble. When you worry you make it double………

But the fact here is that scarcity or lack should not terrify you.

Have you not heard of the world experiencing economic recession, but what do you see today: change!

It is natural to experience lack and also natural for you to learn in the period of lack as you are driven by the challenges you see. Mind you God is not a man that he should lie because, he has set out these times for your good and benefit. Your bad season may be other peoples good season and your good seasons may be other people's bad season. And that is the balance; because life is all about stricken a balance between two equal people.

Keys to minimize lack

Pray God to give you wisdom and understanding

Be Conscious of good times always

Forgive people and be happy and joyous always

Know where you have failed

Think and create new things for yourself

Have faith in God

Avoid continues leaving in sin

I want you to know that forward thinking people are always positioning and repositioning themselves to prosper. This is not a competition but a fact as regards the keys that will be inspiring the natural living that will help you; in your fight for Survival, Resilience and Redemption.

Conclusion

I still want to believe that you have come to realize your full potentials and value as a person through your reading of this priceless book called **" keys for inspiring a successful living: the fastest steps for survival, resilience and redemption".** *May God continue to bless you as you tap and unlock all the supernatural blessing that surrounds you to be successful? Thank you and I love! Jesus is lord.*

References

Anne Frank, The Diary Of A Young Girl, (1942-1944).
Bobby McFerrin, 1988 Hit Song "Don't worry, Be Happy".
Matthias Claudius, We Plough The Field And Scatter, 1782.
Robert Frost, Gods Garden, Robert Frost's Poetry New York, (1969).
The Quotable Einstein, 1996 and *The Expanded Quotable Einstein*, 2000.
San Francisco: Jossey-Bass, 2003.

www.ingramcontent.com/pod-product-compliance
Lightning Source LLC
Chambersburg PA
CBHW072018290526
45787CB00013B/1296